GERMAN SHEPHERDS

FAVORITE DOG BREEDS

Dan Lopez

Norwood House Press

Cataloging-in-Publication Data

Names: Lopez, Dan.
Title: German shepherds / Dan Lopez.
Description: Buffalo, NY : Norwood House Press, 2027. | Series: Favorite dog breeds | Includes glossary and index.
Identifiers: ISBN 9781978580268 (pbk.) | ISBN 9781978580275 (library bound) | ISBN 9781978580282 (ebook)
Subjects: LCSH: German shepherd dog--Juvenile literature. | Dog breeds--Juvenile literature.
Classification: LCC SF429.G37 L67 2027 | DDC 636.7376--dc23

Published in 2027 by
Norwood House Press
2544 Clinton Street
Buffalo, NY 14224

Designer: Rhea Magaro
Editor: Tricia Hoffman

Photo credits: Cover, p.1 anjajuli/Shutterstock.com; p.4 Staff Sgt. Clayton Lenhardt/U.S. Army; p.5 Wikipedia; p.7 Michal Ninger/Shutterstock.com; p.8 Africa Studio/Shutterstock.com; p.9 DTeibe Photography/Shutterstock.com; p.11 Daria Shvetcova/Shutterstock.com; p.13 Newcastle/Shutterstock.com; p.14 Sergii Kumer/Shutterstock.com; p.15 Massimo Todaro/Shutterstock.com; p.17 Amy Lutz/Shutterstock.com; p.19 Fire-n/Shutterstock.com; p.21 anetapics/Shutterstock.com;

Printed in the United States of America

CPSIA compliance information: Batch #CSNHP27: For further information contact Norwood House Press at 1-800-237-9932.

TABLE OF CONTENTS

Meet the German Shepherd

German shepherds are popular pets. Dogs of this **breed** are known for being smart and **capable**. They help police officers, search and rescue teams, and people with disabilities.

In comics, Batman has a German shepherd named Ace the Bat-Hound.

What Do German Shepherds Look Like?

German shepherds are large dogs. They can be 26 inches (66 centimeters) tall. They can weigh 95 pounds (43 kilograms). Their bodies are strong and **muscular**.

These dogs have long **snouts**. Their pointed ears stand up straight. Their tails are long and bushy.

A German shepherd can be tan, black, white, or gray. It is kept warm by a medium-length outer coat and a short, soft **undercoat**.

Where Do German Shepherds Come From?

The name *German shepherd* helps you understand the dog's history. German shepherds were first bred in Germany to **herd** sheep. They can guide as many as 1,000 sheep at a time. They run close to the flock to keep it together and protect it from danger.

How Do German Shepherds Help People?

German shepherds are **loyal** pets. They are friendly to people they know. Always on alert, they make good **watchdogs**.

13

These dogs are highly **intelligent**. They learn new things quickly. Some German shepherds are trained as guide dogs to help people who cannot see.

Many dogs on police and military K-9 teams are German shepherds. These brave dogs sniff out bombs, catch criminals, and find missing people.

POLICE
S. SULESKI
ACCREDITED LAW ENFORCEMENT AGENCY
K-9

What Do German Shepherds Need?

With double layers of fur, German shepherds **shed** a lot. They need to be brushed a few times every week.

German shepherds have lots of energy. They need exercise. They need to stay active, or they will get bored. They enjoy having jobs to do. They love to run and play.

Glossary

breed (breed): one type or kind of an animal

capable (KAY-puh-buhl): able to do things; skillful

herd (hurd): to move animals from one place to another by guiding them

intelligent (in-TEL-i-juhnt): quick to learn and understand; smart

loyal (LOI-uhl): faithful to someone or something

muscular (MUHS-kyuh-lur): having strong muscles

shed (shed): to lose hair or fur naturally

snouts (snouts): the long front parts of animals' heads that include the nose and mouth

undercoat (UHN-dur-koht): a layer of short, soft hair that is underneath an animal's longer outer coat and that provides extra warmth

watchdogs (WAHCH-dawgs): dogs kept to guard property

Thinking Questions

1. Describe a German shepherd's fur.
2. What does it mean to herd sheep?
3. How does a German shepherd's name tell its history?
4. What jobs can German shepherds do?
5. Why do German shepherds need lots of exercise?

Index

About the Author

Dan Lopez is a writer who loves dogs! He has a German shepherd named Hans and an Irish setter named Tam. They love to go for walks in the woods together. Sometimes, they jump in the lake for a swim. Dan lives in Indiana with his wife and three kids.